MW01251070

Praise for Pure Pilgrimage

"A powerful and concise way to stop, take a good look at yourself, and - if you choose - wake up to subconscious patterns that may have been holding you back for years. Chental shares her experiences and insights in a way that can help you rediscover the direction you really want your life to take - and this book helps you now polish the compass to do so."

—Dr Jason Cressey, PhD (Oxford-Psychology), Motivational speaker, and author of *Deep Voices*

"*Pure Pilgrimage* is a truly unique and extraordinary guide to help you discover more about who you really are and how you can truly live a blissful life. With this book I truly believe Chental is revealing ideas that have the potential to truly get you out of dis-empowering emotions and into wonderful feelings of self-love and joy. Enjoy!"

—Peggy McColl,
New York Times bestselling author of *Your Destiny Switch*

"I've welcomed Chental's book into mine and my family's life, and also into the lives of many of my clients. Its liberating message is vital knowledge for all of us. Chental's wisdom is a lifeline to escaping patterns of behaviour that unhappily hold us from ourselves to our self."

—**Jonathan Damonte**, RSHom (NA), CCH, CBT, Homeopath & Bowen Therapist

"*Pure Pilgrimage* is a transformational guide for those seeking to dispel fear and use personal truth as their compass. Chental's seven-step process teaches you to find the freedom you need to unconditionally love yourself and pursue your life's purpose."

—**Steve Olsher**,
New York Times bestselling author of *What Is Your WHAT?*

"*Pure Pilgrimage* is inspiring and helpful. It gives tremendous insight into what spirituality is. Chental reveals the treasures of the ages that are hidden in plain sight within us. For readers seeking truths and spiritual understanding, her teachings overcome resistance to direct divine communication by breaking through ego barriers. The practical exercises help the readers to become self-reliant in solving personal problems and charting a new course for the future. It can transform the readers' life."

—**Dr. Peter Yam**, N.D.

"Chental is a brave and courageous woman, sharing her journey into finding herself with much love and compassion. This book gives clear direction and steps if you are willing to be brave, to find your voice, live authentically, and release yourself from fear. Living on this planet, having this human experience, is a learning process. Living a life joyfully and lovingly is the most beautiful way to spend our time here and one worth working for. Enjoy your journey with this book to living fearlessly and authentically as YOU!"

—**Lisa Sliwowska**, Energy Healer

"*Pure Pilgrimage* is a book that transcends time. Chental Wilson gives us vital life-transforming information that is relatable, full of essential insights, wisdom and empowering processes. Chental interweaves personal and challenging aspects of her own life's journey to demonstrate the ways and means she, herself chose to courageously stay true to herself and her life's purpose. She explains how she did this by listening to her inner guidance that continued to lead her forward, sometimes in challenging times while she stayed compassionately connected to others in her life.

Specifically, Chental's book can assist anyone who wants to break free of areas of residual fear, anger, hurt and unforgiveness and transition towards their own inner wisdom and truth. She does this by providing step-by-step exercises to address these difficult areas. These exercises focus the reader to go beyond fear and move into the strength and vibrancy of our authentic, deeper selves - where we are more powerfully grounded in love.

This book matters, because for every one of us who can be encouraged to more fully and truthfully embrace our uniqueness, from a place of integrity, self-acceptance and compassion - we can then become positive change-makers for ourselves and for others. Being truthful about ourselves can undoubtedly be a life-long journey. In this book, Chental has offered a guiding light."

—**Barbara Halcrow**,

MSW, author of *Ultimate Self-Care* and *Spiritual Intelligence*

Pure PILGRIMAGE

A Journey Back to Self, Using Personal Truth as Your Compass

CHENTAL WILSON

All rights reserved. Thank you for buying an authorized edition of this book and for complying with copyright laws by not reproducing, scanning, including photocopying, recording, taping or by any information storage retrieval without the written permission of the author except in the case of brief quotations embodied in critical articles and reviews.

ISBN: 978-1-9990134-1-7 (Print)
ISBN: 978-1-9990134-0-0 (Ebook)

Front and Back Cover Design by Jessica Wilson
Book Interior and Ebook design by Amit Dey | amitdey2528@gmail.com

www.chentalwilson.com
Instagram
Facebook

This book connects you with an online environment in which the message will continue. You will find expanded content such as audio and video clips, blogs, graphics, pictures, links, and other resources.

Other Books by Chental Wilson

Can I Be Me Without Losing You?

ISBN 978-1-5043-5443-1 Balboa Press

Dedication

This book is dedicated to the late American motivational speaker, author, and publisher Louise Hay (1926–2017) and the awakening heart within each of us.

Louise dedicated her life to helping others. She found her true path from staying on her own compass.

Louise was a beacon of light to me, a candle that never went out. I was fascinated by how she used love to guide her. One evening I picked up her book *You Can Heal Your Life*. I took it into the bath and didn't put it down until I'd finished. I was in awe of how Louise used her own truth as her compass, which led her to unconditionally love herself and others. She had a "knowing" that this would lead her—and it surely did.

How could something as seemingly simple as love lead her? What was her "how"? This is what fascinated me.

Louise created her career from love—first love for herself and then for others. She used love as her compass and went on to create a multimillion-dollar company, publishing people's work and changing lives in a big way. She became the change she wanted to see in the world, and that change continued happening to others.

It was her steadfast belief that truth—delivered from love—is the way.

All done from LOVE, with love and for love.

Thank you, Louise.

Thank you also to the universe for helping me wake up to myself and show me the way.

Thank you to my wonderful daughter Jessica who took the photo for my front cover and designed the front and back cover of my book.

Thank you also to my editors Lorraine Gane, Janet Morrison, and especially Emily Williams for her conscious contribution, in helping me to speak my truth with clarity and compassion so that others may follow their own true compass.

Thank you to my family and friends for always reading and re-reading my book until it was ready to be released.

Thank you to Geoff Affleck and his team, it was so great to finally have a team to lead the way and coach me.

And a final thanks to all my readers for the passion to follow your own compass, it really feels like heaven on earth when you learn to love yourself unconditionally.

Chental xx

Contents

Introduction

This is a journey into the clarity of who you really are.

A compass, pointing north, only gets pulled off its course from magnetic interference. What if we had our own compass and what if we could learn how to navigate from it?

If I told you I've discovered how to tap into my own compass, would you find that intriguing? And would you be interested in learning to do the same? I've discovered that when we live our lives by our own truth and stay on our own "compass course," a door opens into our own consciousness and what comes flooding in is our ability to listen to our guidance system more clearly. Living by your own truth is the step to making this happen.

In living by our truths we fall in love with ourselves again and see we are not separate from anyone or anything. We begin vibrating at a higher frequency and from that higher vibration we have access to universal wisdom and guidance to move forward in our lives. This frequency is *love*. Many ask, "Why can't I hear my own guidance system and guides?"

They have lost the connection to their own heart, to their own compass. They are lost in the confusion of their own mind. Our minds can create emotions that vibrate at lower frequencies, and this takes us further from our truths and joy.

David Hawkins was responsible for calibrating frequencies to vibrations and emotions, which he outlines in his book *Power vs. Force* with a wonderful chart called the Map of Consciousness. I recommend you read it. He shows what our emotions are vibrating at and plots frequencies as they match different emotions. This is how we humans and animals can feel when someone is in fear or love, or even other emotions such as happiness, grief, anger, and so on. Hawkins has it broken down into at least twenty different emotions, so you can see what has been happening. We are feeling others' emotions all the time and it's been confusing us.

We've come into contact with outside interference from other people and situations, and this has created our wounded egos. They are born from living life "off" our own compass and being affected unconsciously by the frequencies of others. This has pulled our own compass off course from living in our own truth. Once you become aware this is happening, there are tools to keep your wounded ego and others from affecting your true compass, but first you need to become aware this is actually happening.

Eastern philosophy puts more importance on the heart, whereas Western philosophy focuses on the mind; however, our deep healing and freedom comes from within the heart.

How do we learn to live by our own true compass? This book is the how-to.

If you're searching for why you haven't been feeling content, at peace or happy with the way your life is going, or if you are just curious to see what living from your truths and being guided by your own compass is all about, this little book may have the answers you have been looking for.

There are no coincidences. The fact that you are holding this book in your hands is guidance from your true compass leading you home, which has already started working.

These secrets have always been inside you. This book is the set of keys to help you unlock ancient secrets that have been dormant for far too long. They'll open the door for you to discover your truest self and help guide you home.

Home is where your heart is. Now, you will discover what that really means.

Why and How I Became a Messenger of Change

I'm going to open with a bold statement.

Do you know there are two of you? Have you heard of Dr. Jekyll and Mr. Hyde, a character (in a book and later a movie) who was one person by day and another by night? All of us, to different degrees, react differently to events in our lives. You may be thinking, "Of course we do," but what I'm talking about here is how we react to everyday events.

A response based from a place of love is received differently than a reaction based from a place of fear. We respond and react to life's events with one of these two different energies. The question to ask yourself is "Which energy am I communicating from at any given time—love or fear?"

What I'm saying is that within each one of us there are two go-to people in our personality. We must become aware of both parts of ourselves. One acts from love and the other reacts from fear. One speaks consciously from our truth, (conscious self) and one from our wounded ego, our shadow (our conditioned self). We all have this inner duality; that's what makes us human. We haven't been taught or realized how it plays out in our lives, and that's why we don't live in our authentic truth and why our relationships and lives may not yet be working for us.

To clarify, this is what I mean by *conditioned self* and *conscious self*: Conditioning comes from those you have interacted with as you grew up, for example, your parents, teachers, family, friends, and so on. This is how your beliefs developed, which are not necessarily what you really believe. You learned things from others and now it's time to ask yourself if this, in fact, is what you really believe. Your *conscious* self knows the truth, for you. When you are out of alignment with your own truth, your body tries to communicate it via illness or emotional pain; it's trying to tell you that your beliefs and thoughts are out of alignment with your own frequency and truth. It's a message to inquire within and find out what's going on. In other words, if your life or health is not flowing in harmony, then this is your cue to go within and be a detective in your own life to find out why. The Universe will create situations and seemingly random events to get you to wake up and pay attention, but if you are not aware, you will miss the messages that come your way every day of your life.

It is complicated at first, but once you understand the duality of yourself, it becomes clear and gets easier to navigate. At the beginning it's hard to catch ourselves as we switch between our dualities, though with practice it will become much easier. Unconditional love has a frequency you can feel. Learning when that shows up is key, because it means in that moment there isn't any fear. This is what we are learning: to release our fears and replace them with love.

This is the important quest for a human: to go in search of oneself, all parts of oneself. I'm pretty sure you weren't taught about the duality within yourself at school. Even though I read many, many books on this concept, about our shadow and our wounded ego, it never dawned on me that I was more in reaction than I was responding. This awareness completely changed my life.

How can you solve a puzzle or a problem in your life if you haven't any idea how or why it's happened or is even happening? The answer: you can't. I'm going to help you to understand the duality within you—where it comes from and why it's there.

It all starts the day we are born. Life takes us on our journey. We believe the journey is a combination of random good and not-so-good events. We may think these events have little guidance from us when anything happens in life, but in truth there is and always has been a master plan, we just didn't know it.

What keeps it even more interesting is that we have free choice. Every time we are faced with a situation, we choose how to handle it and that choice governs our life's path. I was not always aware of my own free choice. I was unconscious. Who was making that choice, me in my truth, (my conscious self) or me in my wounded ego (my conditioned self, my shadow)? You may think making a choice is conscious because it's *your choice*. But it is not necessarily. This was my biggest aha! Before this awareness, I made choices from an unconscious place, because there are two of me. I hadn't been introduced to the other me yet.

You see, life is learned. When you grew up, you were taught certain things; these have either helped or hindered you. We struggle to find our way in life and feel bad when it isn't working out, but in truth we have not been taught the skills. Very few have ever learned how to find their own way. I'm going to show you how to start making conscious choices and start living from your own consciousness—instead of your conditioned self or through others.

Imagine standing in New York City with a map of Vancouver, trying to navigate your way to the Statue of Liberty. You will never find your way, because you don't have the correct map. My whole purpose and passion is to give you the correct map: to teach you how to navigate your own life.

In an interview for his addiction center, Deepak Chopra said, "Yes, you are a victim, no, it wasn't your fault, but now it is your responsibility."

If you want a great life and good health, then it is your responsibility to find out why it's not happening yet. This state requires having an acute understanding and awareness of who you are and how you act in the world around you.

When I approached my late forties, I realized my life had been a kind of consciousness school, and it was time to share what I had learned. Intuitively, I always had a sense I wasn't going to go to a traditional post-secondary school like college or university for these teachings, because life was going to be my teacher. Existence didn't want me to learn the patterns of the generation I grew up in; it wanted to teach me a new way of being. Clearly my life as a conditioned human being wasn't working for me any longer, and I needed to find out why.

I was open to and inquisitive about life's lessons, even when they were hard. And trust me, some were very hard. In my first book, *Can I Be Me Without Losing You?*, I talk in depth about these experiences.

Being human makes it difficult to detach from what is happening to you and those you love. I always wanted to control the outcome of things for others and for myself, to feel safe and relaxed. I used to tell myself I was being kind and helpful, but I discovered in truth I needed to feel safe and calm. And anytime I didn't feel safe and calm, I manipulated situations to get what I needed—peace. I did this because I really believed I was being kind, helpful to others and myself. But I was addicted to peace, an addiction passed down to me by my mother and past generations. After all, women were expected to keep the peace at any cost.

I distinctly remember the day "I" returned to my body with the clear understanding that we are all spiritual beings simply having a human experience. And once we understand this, we are then free to create the life we really want, void of our fears.

This new understanding took away the intensity of life for me. I became relaxed in understanding that this human life I was living was a journey. As spiritual beings we are already perfect, so there isn't a need to try to reach perfection. As human beings, our job is to consciously go on the ride of our human lives, watching and learning and ultimately getting back to knowing where we came from and who we are at our core.

It's the game of remembering. It's time to remember our truths.

Many say we came into the human form to experience separation, that we have all come from a collective oneness. It is also said this was our choice: we wanted to experience separation, so that's the journey we are on. I have experienced separation and I'm happy to say I am back to oneness and I didn't have to die to achieve this awareness.

Now I get to experience heaven on Earth, and you will, too, if you discipline yourself to follow these guidelines and maps I have set out for you. Separation does not feel nice—sometimes it's lonely and dark and cold—but it's necessary to see we have been conditioned to believe things about life and ourselves that simply aren't true and to disperse the illusion that we are separate. Only then can we relax and settle into the time we have left here on Earth, return to oneness and enjoy the ride.

For me, this realization happened about three months after our last child left home. It was a Sunday afternoon much like any other, and I was sitting in my home office watching the ten-part series Oprah Winfrey created with Eckhart Tolle. Watching Oprah Winfrey's talk show, with the enlightened people she interviewed, always brought me closer to finding my true self. Eckhart Tolle had written his second book, called *A New Earth: Awakening to Your Life's Purpose*, and Oprah ended up creating a series with him. On this day, my husband came to the door and asked me a question. I don't remember the question, but I answered him with a voice I didn't recognize. I remember having a sense of him standing there, astonished by my response and becoming angry. I, on the other hand, was still wondering where that voice had come from and whose it was. I pondered a moment and realized I had returned from the depths of my being, from the hold of my personality, to start this new path of becoming me again. I was back, but back from where? It was an incredible feeling of shifting from one reality to another, completely held in limbo, not caring about my current reality but much more interested in the new one I had been thrust into. Where had I gone?

Then a voice within went on to say, "We are not doing this anymore."

I asked, "Who is the 'we' and what are we not doing anymore?"

The voice continued, "We are no longer saying yes when we mean no. Use your truth as your compass, but you must do this with the utmost compassion for your husband, because he will surely not understand. It's time for a new way of communicating."

The whole time I sensed my husband standing in the doorway, and he wasn't happy with my response to his question, but he had no effect on me. I was far too fascinated by what was happening to me. I honestly believe if he hadn't come to the doorway and asked me a question, which broke the vortex I was held in, I would not have had any awareness that this had taken place. I am so grateful he asked that question, whatever it was.

I believe the Universe guided me in that moment and that everything was in perfect alignment. I was directly connected to Spirit. Eckhart Tolle says this happens by grace; it's not something we can force. I believe this journey into truth creates a vibrational frequency of love that opens up the channel through which we can receive this grace. This is why I am so passionate about sharing my experience, because the more authentically you live your life and the more you use your own true compass to guide you, the closer and quicker you will come to being aligned with your truest self within you.

Now, held in this vortex, I was fascinated by this internal dialogue and what seemed like God or a universal truth speaking directly to me. I was told because my job as a parent was complete, it now felt safe for "me" to come out. Why was I hiding? What was I afraid of? What did I want? Who was I? It was as if I had been sleeping for a long time and woke up to find an imposter in my body. Exciting as it was, this was scary, but from that day on I was different. I wasn't able to say yes when I meant no. I used my truth as my compass; it directed me to communicate only from my truth, and it allowed everything out into the open. I became courageous and spoke my truth; I was vulnerable and fearless. Oh, don't get me wrong, it wasn't easy. My physical body could still feel the resistance, but I felt strong enough to move forward. My mantra was "No matter what."

I was now the detective in my own life and determined to understand why I had acted the way I had. What was I so afraid of? It was time to come out of hiding and attend to the next job in my life: to fully understand myself and how I communicated. **How and why had I allowed this imposter to be in the driver's seat of my life?**

I didn't realize I had become someone I was not. When the voice said, "You are no longer saying yes when you mean no," I asked, "Why do I do this?"

The voice answered, "Because you have become just like your mother. You say yes when you mean no for protection, safety and peace."

I realized I had, but how had I not known this before now?

"You watched your mother do this, but it is not who you are. You were never taught how to be in conflict with another. You were never taught about the duality of yourself, the wounded ego. I have come to show you truth, so that you can go on to teach it to others."

Wow, I was fascinated with myself. Could this all be true? It felt so right. I knew it was truth. My whole being resonated with a vibration that felt like I'd come home.

Of course I knew I had made choices in my life, but I had never known until this moment that it was my unconsciousness acting within those choices. My choices, until then, had been made from my conditioned self, my shadow personality, fear—not my conscious self, not my true self, love.

It was as though I had been on autopilot and this voice was revealing my past, present and future. It brought me back to my true self. In that moment I became fearless to speak my truth—100 percent. I had to be authentic. I knew I could never feel truly free and happy unless I followed this path.

The hardest part for me was how to tell my husband, and how to deal with speaking my truth given that he might not like it. I thought I would surely be in conflict, which I had avoided at all costs throughout most of my life. But I knew it was my way forward and I just had to follow my compass, speak my truth with compassion, and trust it would work.

Today, this is my gift to share.

It took a few years to figure out the totality of myself—why and how I had become someone I was not. It was not easy on my husband either, but because he could see this was something I was determined to figure out, he agreed to join me on this journey of rediscovering myself. This was challenging because he was conditioned with his own beliefs from his past (especially from childhood), but I couldn't worry about that. I had to remain on my own path and use my own truth as my compass—and not deviate from this. From the first moment I heard my true voice, I never doubted this was the way. This was a gift, because I had doubted myself before; now I didn't! I realized my husband was in the same duality too. It was like communicating with four people, not just two. You can imagine the conflict. **The fact that I was told to remain compassionate toward my husband was key. I knew he didn't know what I knew—that there were four of us communicating.** In conflict, I now was able to love him deeply because I knew his reactions weren't the real him. His reactions came from his imposter—his wounded ego. Now that I was aware, how could I not have compassion for him? I had been unaware of my own imposter, my own wounded ego within me.

When this happened I had been managing the accounting for my own company for twenty-eight years. It was time for a change. Those four walls and using only one side of my brain was over. I needed to share what life had taught me. I spoke about it to the point at which I could see people were fascinated by my story. They could see from my clarity and passion that I was onto something. My vibration had changed, and I knew people could feel it but they couldn't put it into words.

Before, I had been walking around confused and afraid, therefore my shield of protection had been up and people had felt fear from me. Now, I was free to be me. I didn't need protection anymore. My fear to be me was gone, and my vibration changed to a loving, kind, accepting warmth.

True love doesn't need protection. I let my guard down. I was happy and set free. I healed and was back to being me.

I was encouraged to speak to small groups and others in a bigger way. I decided I must. I felt I had a responsibility to help people understand that it's not just what we say in communication that holds us back from getting in touch with our true selves and what we want in life, it's the energy with which we say it. My hope is for you to also begin to understand what I have discovered as truth.

Shortly after this experience, I needed to get away from all that was familiar to me. I wanted time to plummet further into the unknown of myself, to be more vulnerable, to see how I would do and what more there was for me to understand about what had happened to me.

We decided to sell our house and travel. To my amazement it sold in six weeks, which was unheard of in the market at that time. My husband bought a motorcycle and we toured around the world, visiting thirty countries over fourteen months. Sitting on the back of our bike gave me the opportunity to hear my inner voice even more clearly, without all of life's distractions. I could ask questions all day long and receive answers, and it felt good. I was finally connected to my true self.

I've come to understand that when you can't connect to your intuition, it's because you have allowed life's events and distractions to get in the way and you can't hear your inner voice any longer. It's always there: it always has been, and it always will be.

It's like a radio broadcasting. If you keep transmitting, your mind doesn't allow for any receiving. This is the objective of the wounded ego—to keep you distracted from your true self. It does this because it fears losing control over you. It fears for you and it truly believes it is helping to keep you safe. After all, when you were a young child your ego found ways to protect you from the sadness and cruelty of life, so why wouldn't those same tools work for you today?

I came to love and thank my wounded ego. I cried the day I told it to take the passenger's seat in my life. This felt sad, as though I were grieving the loss of someone special to me, someone I held dear and trusted with my life. I came to understand my ego as my twin soul. Up until this time, it had been in the driver's seat of my life and had protected me, albeit misguidedly. Now it was time for me to be the driver in my own life.

(Remembering this, I am reminded of a Bette Midler song called "Wind Beneath My Wings". To me, the words of this song feel like the ego is thanking the true self for letting it be part of its life, it's like the ego is saying thank you.)

I grew up. I understood the totality of my life. I realized I had been navigating most of my life from a place of fear and sadness; although I had felt love in my heart, my fear had won over my love. When I was in fear, I couldn't see that I allowed my wounded ego to communicate for me. And yet when I was feeling loved and safe, I communicated from my true self. Allowing your wounded ego to communicate for you will never result in the life you truly want. It's a misguided form of communication and not love.

Few people get to sit for hours and hours and watch the world go by as they travel across new countries. My inner voice spoke to me often, filling me with the joy of life and all the endless possibilities in store for me. It was as if I had tapped into my fairy godmother and all my wishes could be fulfilled, and yet all I was doing was sitting on the back of that bike. It was like being in a different reality. I asked questions and received answers. I had found the open channel that most of us only get small tastes of throughout our lives. I didn't have any thoughts of shopping, money management, making dinners, groceries, meetings, and so on—only the joy of simply being with my husband on our motorcycle and being myself. It was a feeling of complete freedom, finally experiencing what life and living is supposed to feel like—not to mention realizing how incredibly awesome humans really are. (The details of this journey will be featured in my third book, *A Pillion in a Million*. Look for it soon!)

When our trip ended, I found myself back home, thrust into the reality of my old physical life. My mind threw in doubts of whether I could do what I had been asked to do: write a book and share. To be even more vulnerable, not just with my partner but with the world. The world would know what I was thinking. Did I have enough to say and share? Questions came up as to whether I was qualified or even worthy enough. It was so interesting. On the back of the bike I didn't have any doubts whatsoever, and yet back in my old life and about to embark on my first book, my outdated beliefs started to creep back in.

Now I was about to be vulnerable with the public, my family and my friends. People I saw every day would know everything about us. You can imagine the fear, but I knew I had to do it. This was another level of me I had to get to know.

I remembered reading Anita Moorjani's book *Dying to Be Me*, in which she talked about going to India after being diagnosed with cancer. Her guru told her she didn't have cancer. She stayed with him for three months and returned home cancer free! But a year later the cancer returned. You see, as Bruce Lipton, biologist and author, says, our environment plays a major role in our health. I'm not talking only about our physical environment but also our mental environment. The same was true for me. Physically, I was back in my old surroundings and I was watching myself re-enter my old life. I had learned to be a detached observer of myself and now I was being tested once again. I wondered, "Can I be me, all of me, with this book? Can I speak my truth and accept the consequences of that?"

Fortunately, by this time I was aware of these thoughts running through me. I realized I could do anything, and the only thing that had stopped me before was the beliefs I had taken on from my conditioning, which I had believed to be true. Once I saw that my true self was and always has been capable of whatever I put my mind to (free of the doubts and old beliefs of my past), I knew this was my next move:

to become a messenger of change. I had cleared the pathway to share my gift fearlessly, so I wrote my first book, *Can I Be Me, Without Losing You?*

The discovery I made: the only thing stopping people from being true to themselves, sharing their message, and becoming messengers of change is their own old belief patterns, doubts, and stories they are still holding onto. Once we recognize what these actually are, we can change and align them with what we want to do and be in our life. We can start to live our lives from our own truths.

Can you imagine the life you could be living right now with all the doubts and old beliefs gone and out of your way? You would be living a fulfilling life and have the courage to finally share your own message and your true self with the world. You would allow others to live their lives, and that's the best gift one person can give to another. I encourage you, whatever your inner voice is whispering, say yes. Own your voice and your gift to become a messenger of change and share yourself and your message with all of us.

As I mentioned, one message I heard on the back of the bike was that I was going to write a book and participate in public speaking engagements. When I got back home it all started to unfold. A friend of mine invited me to visit for a weekend. She said a publisher who only published books of influence was coming to give a talk, and off I went. The publisher and I hit it off, and the next thing I knew I was taking a three-day workshop with her and a group of seven other new writers.

At first, I was shy and nervous about sharing my message. I felt super vulnerable, but as the days wore on, I loved it. Over the next year, I sat down every day to write. The name of an editor came across my desk twice, so I met with her and she turned out to be the perfect match. It was as if once I made the decision to write, existence provided the tools I needed to complete my book. It was tough going, because at the same time I was renovating my house and taking a year off work, so money was tight, but I persevered, and eighteen months later *Can I Be Me, Without Losing You?* was released on Amazon!

I transcended my fear to speak my truth, and today I'm not afraid to get up on stage and expose my every thought in public. This is clearly my life's job: to share my story and become a messenger of change for clearer, fearless, detached, and more honest communication. If I'd been asked several years back to get up on stage in front of people and speak, I would not have been able to do it. After my experience, I realized I was shown the way to share it with others. Now I can't wait to get up there and share! This message to be true to yourself is so important and I can't keep it a secret.

I have listened to hundreds of messengers of change, and the one thing we all seem to have in common is the experience of hearing an inner voice whispering to us to go forward with an idea. Many doubt themselves because of their conditioning. My message: don't listen to the voice that says you aren't smart enough, good enough, worthy enough, or even have something important to say. I say you do; go for it. The voice that expresses doubt is the wounded ego struggling to protect you and stay in control of your life because of fear, but you don't need protection any longer—move through those fears and into love.

If you have been hearing this voice, understand that any doubts, fears, or beliefs are just simply that, old stories from your conditioning—they are not true. Choose to let go of them, live fearlessly and become a messenger of change for yourself, your family, and the world. This is how one person can make a difference. This is how the world will find peace.

There are only two directions in which we steer our lives: one is to love and the other is to fear. Ask yourself at any given time which one are you operating from. Fear comes from the ego's need for control and from our wounds; it cannot exist where love and truth are in harmony.

Together we can create the ripples of change our world so desperately needs to heal. For encouragement, I encourage you to connect with yourself, with me, and with others who have gone before you and join us in becoming messengers of change.

There is one saying I still hold true from my past: Charity begins at home. As I traveled the world, although I felt pulled by the injustices against people in some of the countries I visited, this made me realize I can make a difference in my own backyard. By leading a conscious life, I affect my family and friends and those I come into contact with along the way; thus, the universal wisdom does affect everyone around me.

One person can make a difference! I encourage you to start today, become your truest self, give consciousness to the messenger within, and share your gift with those you love and our world.

The tool is simple: it's truth. The journey isn't for the faint of heart, but it is so worth it.

I often find inspiration in music. I encourage you to take a few minutes to listen to *Change* by Tracy Chapman. I feel like it is the perfect song to welcome you into the work that lies ahead.

I have tried to keep this book short because we are bombarded with self-help books that just seem to confuse us further. I have used the tools I was shown and the method I was told. Good luck on your journey.

Chental x

Stepping Into Your Truth

By following these teachings and exercises, you will build tools for peaceful communication within relationships, including, most importantly, the one with yourself. I encourage you to designate a notebook for the following exercises so that you may reflect back on your answers as we move forward.

For those embarking on this journey—remember the following:

- Actions speak louder than words.
- Do not hold on to past mistakes, learn from them.
- You are love.
- From love you can take your next step as a new person. All you have to do is be willing, let go and trust.
- Don't cling to old ways. Walk bravely. Many will question your sanity, even those who have been close friends. You are stepping out of the ordinary mindset and this makes others uncomfortable.

- Shame and blame do not have any place for the work we are doing here, and there can't be any judge present.

- Awareness is the key. Bring your curiosity, courage, truth, and compassion for yourself and others.

Many times we will talk about things, but from witnessing our actions we will know whether we are communicating from our true selves (love) or our conditioned selves (fear). It is this energy others will feel—truth has its own frequency, as does fear. The frequency of fear will take you off your compass and others off theirs, too. Love allows each person to stay on their own compass.

My job as a 'consciousness' coach is to reflect back to people what they can't see for themselves. Once they understand the duality of love and fear within themselves, they start to watch for it—and in this watching they become conscious of it. I reflect back (to them) when they are acting from the ego (fear) or from truth (love). I can read the signs, I can feel their energy changes, and I can help them become aware for themselves. In truth, we were all born with the ability to read the energy of others; as young children, we didn't understand the words sometimes, but we felt the energy. This is why we have not been able to be our true selves as adults: another's fear has become our fear and it controls us. Fear controls us and we become controlling because of fear. We have become unconscious with regard to our ability to read fear and love; now it's time to bring it back as a tool into our conscious awareness.

If acting from your truth seems uncomfortable, then start by following your joy. The vibration of joy is a step in the right direction. This will help you find truth. When we vibrate at the level of joy and an experience happens that brings that vibration down, we don't feel well. This is a sign to speak your truth, whatever that is. But remember, deliver it with compassion—this is key.

Albert Einstein said, "You cannot use the same mind that created the problems to solve them." As you learn to listen and identify your truths, you will learn to discern which voice to listen to and become the master of your own life.

LET THE HEART SPEAK

STEP ONE

Awareness Using Truth

To begin, let the following questions lead you into an awareness of your truth. While working through these answers, try to pretend you are the only person in the world. Everyone else is here to help you to evolve—even though they seem to be making things difficult for you. In answering these questions, speak your truths. I don't want you to feel afraid of what you'll write. Be brave. The braver you are on this journey, the faster you will get to see the core of where your pain and suffering is coming from. Give yourself permission to empty out your feelings on paper without judgment. Courage is required to step into all of you: let courage be your guide at this point. Remember my mantra, "No matter what, I will write my truth."

EXERCISE I

If anything has triggered you so far, write down the words that initiated the awareness. Identify what being triggered feels like (this will help you build the awareness).

What needs to happen for you to feel free and at peace in yourself and your life? If you struggle with this question, think of what makes you feel peaceful or at peace. Use the following bullet points to guide you:

- Who is with you?
- Are you alone?
- Where are you?
- What are you doing?
- What is not happening?
- What is not there?

The answers will guide you to see what you believe needs to happen for you to feel free and at peace.

EXERCISE II

Take a blank page in your notebook and draw a line down the middle. For one heading write, "What gives to me?" and for the other heading write, "What takes from me?" These can be either people or things, e.g., "My husband takes from me when he is unhappy that I'm home late and tells me this or questions why" or "My husband gives to me when he is waiting for me with herbal tea when I get home!" Write at least ten to fifteen points on each side, as this will help you to identify what is bringing you joy and what is taking from your joy. Don't forget, it can be anything: diet, exercise, work, friends, family, etc. We are trying to determine what is using up your energy and keeping your ego engaged.

EXERCISE III

Reflect on what you have written so far, and use it as a guide to complete the following sentence:

- I believe I need [insert answers] to happen for me to feel free and at peace.

Write down all the answers that come to you, and number them as you go. If it's easier, you can start with the opposite question:

- Currently, what is happening in my life that is making me feel off-balance, upset, angry or sad?

Sometimes it's easier to express what is making us feel upset or angry, especially if we feel off course. After that, go back to the previous question. We are just identifying at this time what we are feeling in the energy.

Building an awareness of how you lose track of yourself will become the guide to how to get back to your own compass course. If it is a person, don't think you will have to remove this person from your life, because that is not necessary most of the time. It's our belief about the situation that makes us think this; it isn't necessarily true, so don't worry or go into any fear. As I was working with my partner and learning to speak my truth, I had already come to detachment. In other words, I knew I had to be me. If he didn't like the authentic me, then he would have to figure out what to do about that to stay on his own compass.

When I instruct people to speak their truth, they often ask, "How do I know what my truth is?"

I say, "If you were the only person in the world, what would your answer to any question be?" It would be your truth! There would not be any reason for you not to speak your truth, because there would not be any consequences in doing so.

We know our truth but seldom speak it. Why? We are afraid of the consequences. One step on this journey is for you to become comfortable tapping into and speaking your truth.

Be aware of every time you don't speak your truth. You will feel this as fear. You may notice a heightened awareness in your body, and fear will get you to compromise yourself. For example, whenever my partner asked me, "What time might you be home?" I used to guess at a time I thought he would be okay with, instead of telling him the real time I would likely be home. I did this because I believed if I told him the later time, then he would get upset with me, and I didn't like that feeling. So, I would tell him the earlier time, which was not true and set him up for further disappointment.

This step toward consciously becoming your authentic self by speaking your truth, and developing that awareness, will eventually set you free. When you go against your truth, your body is aware and weakens. Kinesiology is the science that explains how truth affects your muscle tissue. Unfortunately, the mind thinks you can avoid truth and tries, but health issues arise when you listen more to the mind than to your truth.

Fear

Your truth comes from love of self. When you are afraid to speak your truth, the conditioned self - fear -gets summoned. This conditioned self doesn't know what is best for you, but it will try to convince you it does. Relationships break down because we have learned and become conditioned to miscommunicate our truth; we are not aware of who is actually communicating in any given moment—is it truth or the frightened self? This is the duality within each one of us, and unless we become aware of this duality, we will not find peace in ourselves or for our planet.

Extremely frightened people are called narcissists because they only operate from fear. They have become so afraid that they have disconnected from their true selves, and any attempt to reconnect them usually is not helpful because they are in extreme fear. They don't believe there is a self, and to say the conditioned self is an imposter in their lives is to say they won't exist, because they believe they are the conditioned self. It's extremely sad because they are so disconnected from themselves; these people have locked away their hearts so they can't be hurt again. If you are dealing with someone in your life who is often in reaction, this shows they are in some kind of fear. The only way to reach them is to become fearless yourself and live in your own truth—with compassion for them. To do this, you need to know yourself first. Becoming aware of why you act the way you do is a step toward finding your truth.

When we love others deeply, we believe if we just keep loving them, one day they will wake up and break through the illusion of themselves, but this is not true. You can't help others see themselves by just loving them. The only way to help other people see who they really are is to live this yourself. Love yourself enough to be true to yourself and speak your truth. When you learn to deliver your truth with compassion, others will receive this energy and not go into fear. The problems happen when we try to deliver our truths but are still in fear. This just puts the other person into more fear, which makes for confusing communication and usually doesn't result in a resolution—not because there can't be one, but because we don't understand what's happening in our energy.

As you become more aware of yourself, you will change, and in this change others don't have any other choice but to change. One day they will also see who they really are, because of the changes in you. We reflect to one another. Love reflects more love, fear reflects more fear.

To reiterate, the belief that you can help others by loving them and compromising yourself just isn't so—the only way to help others is to wake up first. Unless you have walked the path back to your own truth of who you are, you cannot lead another.

My partner was the catalyst for my evolution. I had to step into my own truths and power for me to be free. When I stopped focusing on how I could help him, I realized I had to be me, no matter what.

Bruce Lipton, the author of *Spontaneous Evolution: Our Positive Future*, says, "When your conscious mind has a belief that is in conflict with a formerly learned 'truth' (belief) stored in the subconscious mind, the intellectual conflict expresses itself as a weakening of the body's muscle."

He goes on to say, "It is not our genes but our beliefs that control our lives and our health." It certainly was in my case. My fear to speak my truth showed up in overworked adrenals, leaving me feeling tired and depressed and dealing with back injuries.

Beliefs come from our conditioning. Once we understand we have the power to change our beliefs, then we can start living our lives from our truths. To change our beliefs or review them, we first need to know what we believe from our true selves, and what we believe from our conditioned selves (the stories we make up in our heads that may not be true). This is the detective work.

The magic is when you are the safest person for you to be around. You will never feel unsafe around another person again, because you will always be with you. The only reason another person can make you feel unsafe is because you are not yet the safest person for you to be around. Which is another way of seeing how often you say "I love you" to yourself—there's the evidence.

"I'd love to love myself, if only I had time," is something Matt Kahn describes in his talk, *Love is the Only Answer*. This is all too familiar.

"We always have things to do, problems to fix. What if I was to tell you that in your...reality, the world you see and the *you* as a person are both one and the same energy? Your distractions are manifesting tangible, justifiable reasons why you still don't have time to give you the loving attention that you never learned how to give yourself. Until we love ourselves, we manifest all sorts of reasons why we still don't have time to love ourselves." -*Love is the Only Answer*, Matt Kahn.

Matt confirms how loving yourself will set you free. (Check out his talk online at this link.)

EXERCISE IV

Watch yourself in communication with others.

This will take some time and reflection. To start, watch your breathing and the breathing of others. If others seem angry or anxious, rather than focusing on their words, watch their breath. See if you can hold a space for them from a place of love and compassion and then breathe in a relaxed state yourself. In other words, try to bring your breathing into alignment with how you feel when you are safe and feeling love. Even though you may not feel safe, try to redirect the energy back to love. Others will follow your breath because their ego will be confused as to what's happening in your energy. You won't be feeding their ego. What their ego wants is conflict, because it's in fear, but you will be feeding it love. The ego cannot survive and stay in fear when love is present. The ego only becomes present when fear rises.

I observed my partner when he was angry. He would say he was not angry but frustrated, yet I would feel his frustration as anger and an attack on me. In time, I learned to see he was twice as afraid as I was in communication with me, and this awareness helped me to be compassionate toward him. I could never be angry at someone in more fear than me. I had to understand my fear was triggering his fears. If I could switch from fear to love, I could help him do the same, and speak my own truth more easily. This takes practice, but it doesn't take long to see the results. I had to learn to trust myself to do this. I had to know I could stand up for myself in my truth.

As you observe yourself, write down when you witness yourself not speaking your truth. Ask yourself, "Why aren't I speaking my truth?" and "What do I believe will happen if I do?" Take time to write down your thoughts from each experience. It is helpful to revisit your answers.

This is your first lesson in awareness. I want you to get to know why you can't or won't or don't speak your truth.

Internal Work

I don't advise verbalizing or sharing what you have come to (at this point) with others. This is internal work, and sharing may only confuse you. Do this for as long as you feel necessary before taking the next step. I recommend a couple of weeks of working alone, because you can be more honest with some people in your life than with others. You are learning about yourself and why you communicate the way you do.

You will feel many emotions arising at this time. Write a description of what they bring up for you. For example, mine was "I can't speak my truth because the consequences are too frightening to me. I'll just retreat. I will get in trouble. People won't like me. I'm protecting my kids. I won't have peace. I'm afraid."

Keep going. The deeper you go, the clearer it becomes. Remember, no one is reading your answers. It's only you and your wounded self. If you're feeling afraid to write, just allow that feeling to come in; it's okay and expected. Work toward writing all your thoughts down in detail.

We live in duality for most of our lives. This work aligns and brings awareness into these two parts of ourselves we otherwise might never have become aware of. We need to become aware of the two of us, then we can choose how to move forward in how we communicate and how we make choices. We can only get to know our wounded self if we have a keen awareness of how we communicate, so this step is about watching yourself with others. It's as though there's a "you" watching "you" and others communicate.

Now you can observe and recognize how often you are not speaking your truth due to fear of the consequences, and what those fears are. Identifying your fears is the number one step, because fear controls and is a controller.

In other words, when you are in fear you become controllable, and by the same token, when you feel afraid you control others, by putting them in fear with the negative energy you project. This is why the journey to become fearless is important. We do not want to live our lives in fear and thereby be controlling or be controlled. This is stressful and will lead to health issues, and could even influence future generations with unnecessary negative conditioning. Children brought up by narcissistic (fear-based) parents often become narcissist themselves or get into relationships with other narcissists, not because they truly love them or their behavior but because it's familiar to them. They learned how to navigate this type of personality from a young age; it makes them feel in control because they're familiar with how to navigate it. Unfortunately, it also means they can't live in their own truth, because it won't be allowed or tolerated. It's a misguided view of what love is.

If we don't do this work for ourselves, we run the risk of these patterns repeating for generations to come. This is how we can make a difference. We teach others and our children by how we act, not by what we say. People pick up on energy and build their beliefs from actions, not words. Words come after the feeling, so it's important to be mindful of your thoughts, which are creating your energy. This is picked up by others around you—it's what they feel.

How often do you know things about people even if they haven't told you anything? You are picking up their energy, their vibrations. Our bodies are clever and always communicating, and we do this without speaking. Use the new awareness you build from these exercises to be conscious of the energy you present, and of that which is presented to you. Reflect on it, and when you feel fear, see if you can discover where it is coming from, yourself or another.

Compassion

What is compassion? It is the heart's ability to be completely vulnerable, so that you can be present. Compassion happens when you have the awareness to recognize what fear is and where it's coming from.

Only when compassion is present can people speak their truth.

If speaking your truth is your first priority, then delivering it with compassion is your second. **This is key**. You have to train yourself to do this. Most people are able to speak some truth, but it's usually delivered from a place of "I'm done and I've had enough, so now I'm going to tell you the truth." This is not compassion. This type of delivery happens when you believe the other people are aware and should be able to receive your truth, but they are not aware of the energy that's being communicated because they have not done the same work as you. This type of communication triggers another's ego into fear because that is what they are feeling—your fear. Have compassion for yourself and others, knowing you, too, have been unaware in the past. Compassion is knowing we all make mistakes. Be understanding, and from your heart, send out love. Love cannot coexist with fear. Fear has to subside before love returns, and someone has to build this awareness.

These communication challenges are frustrating because you may be aware of the unconsciousness of others but they are not yet aware. Your own wounded ego tries to tell you you're right and entitled to this delivery, but it's just not helpful. The real breakthrough comes when your delivery (your truth) is spoken from a grounded place and a belief in self—a "no matter what" belief, but with the utmost compassion for others. You must remember that they do not understand. They cannot see themselves. This assertive style speaks volumes to their wounded egos. Their egos are ready for battle, and if you refuse to engage and remain in your truth and integrity, their wounded egos have no choice but to stand down. When your energy communicates no fear of speaking your truth and is delivered with compassion, then their egos will have no choice but to stand down, and you will feel the difference in their energy. You may even witness their energy "spin" because it has no place to disperse but to the self. You no longer will absorb the fears of others. You are no longer a sponge for their misguided energy.

Most of the time when conflict arises from one person trying to speak their truth, it's because it puts the other one in fear. Both people are try-ing to defend their positions. If you try defending your truth, it tells the other person's ego there is still a chance of winning, so it's best not to defend your-self—just speak your truth. This is such an important step if you want others in your life to receive your truth without going into fear.

I shared a piece in my first book that reminds me of the feeling when you just don't want to fight anymore. You have come to a place where you are tired and just need nurturing and love, a place of sur-render. It's not the same as giving up. What's happen-ing is your ego is standing down. The ego begins to realize you are taking control and responsibility, and little by little it starts to surrender to your true self.

This quote from my first book is by Chief Joseph (1840?–1904) of the Nez Percé in Northeast Oregon. It encapsulates the Native American experience of surrender, and describes the point I got to in my own exhaustion. I became fearless, my ego stood down, and I no longer wished to manipulate or control or be controlled; I just wanted to be me. I was tired and done.

> "Our chiefs are dead; the little children are freezing to death. My people have no blankets, no food. ... I want to have time to look for my children and see how many I can find. ... Hear me, my chiefs, I am

tired. My heart is sick and sad. From where
the sun now stands, I will fight no more."

This paragraph spoke to me strongly. It simplified
that all I had to do was speak my truth. I had over-
complicated my thoughts. It taught me to get out
of my mind and speak what is clearly in my heart
without the fear of being judged, to ask for what I
need, just to say my truth. I had overanalyzed every
thought, and why? I had tried to find a way in which
peace would and could prevail, which in some cir-
cumstances I now knew just couldn't happen—at
least, not the way I wanted it to. There is peace and
intimacy hiding in conflict, and I needed to understand that. This was a big lesson for me: this had been
my fear all my life.

I knew to speak my truth would evoke the
wounded ego in others, and that terrified me. I would
do anything to prevent that from happening, which
included compromising myself. I never realized all
I had to do was speak my truth, without fear and
with compassion for others. I finally realized I had to
stick up for myself and say, "No more. I will fight no
more, I am done." This was the beginning of living
my life as my truest self. Had I been taught this as
a young girl, I could have been me a long time ago.

STEP THREE

Detachment

etachment from the reactions of others is required to do this work. Many will think detachment is "not loving," but it is the complete opposite. Once you are able to achieve this, only then will you find the courage to speak your truth. As you learn to love and respect yourself, it will become easier to speak your truth with detachment: with awareness comes consciousness. Remember, learning to unconditionally love yourself is the work we are doing. Compassion arises for others when you can become compassionate toward yourself. When you learn your actions and reactions have come from your fears and conditioning, not your truth, you will become more compassionate toward yourself and others. If you find yourself judging or defending yourself, you know you still have work to do around your own fears. There is no judgment in this work, just observation.

Remember: What you don't know, you don't know, until you know, and then you know. So, no blame, no shame!

EXERCISE V

Fact: Fear stops us from speaking our truth.

It's the reactions of others that stop you from speaking your truth, because their fear (reactions) frightens you. Or it can be that your fear also stops you because the consequences of speaking your truth put them into fear. Either way it's fear. Fear is F.E.A.R.: False-Emotions-Appearing-Real.

Fear feels real because it's an energy. When you understand you can breathe, let fear go, and return to love, all within a few seconds, then this becomes your tool. It feels like magic when it happens, because the ego, remember, can only exist if fear is present. Fear is like food to the ego. Once love comes in as an energy form, the ego steps aside. Love needs no protection, so as an energy form, the ego doesn't need to be present, because the ego is only there when we are in fear.

Triggers

Watch yourself again and document in your notebook how you feel when others trigger you. What are you feeling? Have you been considered, heard, respected, overruled, controlled, and so on? Keep writing until you feel you have emptied your thoughts. Remember to breathe.

It's very important to determine what triggers you. When you're triggered, your wounded ego steps in quickly and tries to come to your rescue. It's responding to your fear; that's how it knows to wake up. Most of the time, our wounded ego sits waiting for the moment it's required, and when you are in fear it wakes up. You can feel it in your body as adrenaline. At this time, watch and become aware of what's happening in your body. Be aware of what you say. Observe yourself. Don't stop speaking your truth, even though it may get you into trouble, just observe how you are feeling. Watch how you deliver your truth and another's response. Write the experience down to study at a later date. Being in fear too often for too long drains your body, and it is my belief this is what leads to adrenal fatigue and then to depression, among other health issues. You are learning to observe and detach from your feelings.

We as humans are not aware of this dance between fear and love as it is going on. Before I was aware, if I had been asked if I was in fear or if I was afraid, I would have defended myself by saying I wasn't, but that wasn't true. I just wasn't aware of the energy in my body changing from love to fear. When you switch from love to fear, you become unconscious. With fear present, it's very difficult to remain aware of your duality, because fear is taking up your immediate attention with a fight-or-flight response. You are transmitting outward and not going inward. It will take practice to become a witness to yourself while you are in fear.

Ideally, and eventually, you won't need to react or defend yourself. Just watch. If you do react, watch that too. Tell yourself all is well, you are safe, it will all work out, and breathe. You are learning the art of "people whispering," using your energy to dissipate your fear and in turn another's fear, so you can speak your truth.

Continue to watch your body and write down how it's feeling whenever you can. Remember, this is all about watching. Don't judge yourself even if you do react or become defensive, because judgment blocks your ability to go further. Be kind and tell yourself you are learning. You are beginning to understand and see when fears belong to you or to another, and you are on the path to detachment.

This lesson helped me to understand why I was in fear. Sometimes the fear didn't originate from me; it had come to me from others. I felt their fear, which put me in my own fear and made me doubt myself even more, which was very confusing. This pulled me off my own compass.

Confusion arises in communication because we don't understand what's happening in the mix of energy and we don't know who creates the fear first. It's impossible to discern without awareness. Energy is felt long before the words are spoken, and this is confusing. I never realized I was carrying fear from my husband's reactions to my truth. I used to believe he was in fear, and he was, but I came to understand I initiated the situation with my own fear before delivering my truth. It was coming from me. Fear was in me, which then triggered his fears. Ugh! At times he would be doing the same thing to me, and this is what we came to understand.

However, I only had control over my own fear. That's all we can do: control our own fears. The magic is when we learn to dissipate our own fear and walk courageously toward what frightens us. It gives others permission to do the same, and eventually fear doesn't show up. Or if and when it does, it leaves as quickly as it arrived because now we know what's really happening. The situation is back within our control.

When another person triggers you, you go into fear and your body releases adrenaline. This is a physical built-in mechanism to help you fight off danger. Most times you are not in physical danger, but the body doesn't know this. Your body does not know how to discern the difference between physical safety and emotional safety, so it treats the threat the same. Once that adrenaline is released, it takes approximately ninety seconds to dissipate throughout your body. Your body feels a heightened sense of awareness and wants to react. Resist the temptation. Wait ninety seconds and then act. This will take practice, though you will see it makes a big difference in your ability to communicate from a conscious level. Breathe. While you are in this reaction of ninety seconds, you are unconscious, you are in fight or flight. This is when people have panic attacks. The feeling sends them into more fear because they feel out of control, when in fact it's just the body releasing adrenaline because they have gone into fear.

Imagine if people knew this was happening. They could train themselves to breathe and thereby dissipate the fear and not panic. Reacting comes from our unconsciousness, it comes from our fears and is often very frightening. Fear feels real, it can feel like we are losing control.

Knowing I could control my own fear was a big *aha*! moment for me. I could ground myself, be fearless, and still deliver my truth without worrying about the reactions of others.

The ability to ground yourself happens when you understand what fear is. Fear is a feeling that only persists because you keep feeding the story, thereby creating more fear.

My ability to ground myself and see not only my fear but my partner's fear also allowed for his truths to surface because he wasn't afraid of me, as I wasn't generating fear any longer. It wasn't in the words, it was in the energy. I don't know about you, but no one taught me that our energy gets released long before our spoken words and that energy is the first thing we communicate with.

Given a choice, most people would rather preserve their relationships than stop their suffering, because it's hard work. These tools are simple but very difficult to put into action, because we were not taught how to speak our truth. We were taught to avoid conflict, and thereby, we didn't learn to speak our truth. Now we know that speaking our truth, delivered with compassion, is what we are changing.

Let's take a moment to review what we have discussed so far.

The First Three Steps to Transformation

- Awareness: Learn to identify what you are feeling—love or fear—and how they feel different in your body.

- Compassion: Once you've identified what you're feeling, and built awareness, you can work on switching from fear to love, and your delivery will naturally become more compassionate.

- Detachment: Realize you cannot fix anyone else; that is their decision to evolve or not. By becoming aware of your own fear-versus-love energy and having compassion toward others who don't yet understand, you find acceptance - and, in that, detachment. It no longer becomes about anyone else but yourself. In truth, to think anyone else needs fixing means you don't accept them as they are - and this is a judgment.

These three steps form the foundation of becoming a conscious communicator. Your fears, whether you know them or not, are never going to help you communicate and reach the outcome you wish. Learn what your fears are and bring compassionate understanding to them, then learn to dissipate them. Awareness with action is how transformation happens.

This is transforming the unconscious into consciousness, working through your fears, and understanding what fear is and how it feels in the body.

Once this is done, the energy can never be unconscious again. It's like learning to ride a bike; you can't unlearn how to do it.

Long-lasting transformation happens after awareness, once you take the action to speak your truth. Without action, it's still an idea, one your ego can throw doubt on. What I want is for you to have an experience using an action, using truth. As soon as you can, find a situation in which you can take action using truth (this is Step Four).

The biggest surprise to me during my transformation was recognizing that I was the puppeteer, causing the difficult communications a lot of the time through my inability to see that I was bringing fear energy into my communications. I was also surprised by my lack of awareness regarding this: I was in fear myself.

Fear lies deep within us, and although I believed I had all the right words, until I was ready to face my own fears, I kept them hidden, even from myself. Or at least my ego did. The ego can be so convincing. Our biggest work is to discern when we are acting from the ego (fear) and when we are acting from truth (love). Once you learn to feel the difference in the vibration these energies carry, it becomes easy.

I ask myself on a daily basis, "Am I at LOVE or above? If not, why not?" By doing this, I fine-tune my awareness and keep myself in check daily.

If you tend to fall unconsciously and easily into conflict, then this book will help you also. The only reason you choose conflict to communicate is because you want to control, because you have a fear of something. Please don't ever judge yourself. Dig deep and find out what your fear is. If you find people say, "It's not what you say, it's how you say it …," then this is a good indication that you tend to go toward conflict when you communicate. This simply means you go into fear, which in turn wakes up the ego to come to your defence, so the ego can stay in control. By the same token, however, the way that I handled fear was to say 'yes' when I really meant 'no' because I was afraid of conflict and losing my inner sense of peace.

So, both ways of handling fear are about the fear of losing control - they just look different.

The ego does this to protect you and uses it as a form of control to help you feel safe; however, it's not going to help you. This is the work of the wounded ego. Don't get mad at it for trying to protect you; there was a time in your life when you needed this. Now you are an adult and it's time to fully understand what's been happening and to recognize the duality within yourself.

Conflict is very often misunderstood. There is intimacy in conscious conflict, when you are aware of yourself, your fears, and your energy during the conflict. I was so happy to be able to feel this again in my relationship. Once we became fearless to speak our truths, intimacy returned. Before, I didn't feel like being intimate when I was in fear all the time.

Those who live with narcissist-type personalities know their energy, which is anxious and frightening. What you will come to understand is they are twice as afraid as you are, and it comes out as anger and a need to control. They are in extreme protection. It appears they are thinking only about themselves, but what is really happening is they believe they are in some kind of danger. Narcissists wear masks (the wounded ego mask), and if you threaten their intelligence (however big or small), you will get the same reaction: the wrath of the ego. Their reaction is usually aggressive, because they have never connected to their self and they are afraid. They believe if you manage to remove their mask, they will be left with nothing, no identity, and they can't allow that to happen. It is likely they lost their connection to self as children. They have been living their life in fear.

It is possible to help them with your own fearless energy. This was my mission: How do I eliminate my own fears and how can I help my partner eliminate his—without being an enabler or compromising my own truths? When I had my *aha*! moment while watching Eckhart with Oprah, I remember being told, "Not only are you stopping your own evolution by not speaking your truth, but you are also stopping your partner's evolution because no awareness is happening for either of you. Without awareness, consciousness cannot be." Once I heard that, I knew I had to stop being an enabler.

STEP FOUR

Action

EXERCISE VI

When you feel you have a good understanding of the previous steps, start step four by asking your partner or a friend the following question (you can use your own words):

- Can you hold a sacred and safe place for me to grow, to come to know myself better so I'm able to love myself and you and others on a deeper level? In other words, will you help me become a detective in my life to find out why I do the things I do? Will you provide a safe place for me to heal?

When both people can do this, it's wonderful. If the other doesn't or can't do this, don't worry, you can still choose to participate—that is your responsibility. Remember, others don't have to do any work on themselves for you to become you. There is a trap in believing someone else has to change for you to be your authentic self. This is only giving your power away. You don't have to wait for anyone else for you to be you. The wonderful thing about asking this is that you will see if their ego goes into fear or if they respond with kindness and a willingness to help you. Again, don't worry about them; this is about you.

Just before I surrendered to this practice, I heard my ego trying to trick me. I felt a lot of fear and thought it was real, even when I knew I could control it. Be aware that throughout all of these lessons, the ego will be present and you will feel a level of fear. This is normal, but just know fear is what will trigger the ego to wake up. The difference is it doesn't have to be in control. That's up to you, with your new level of awareness. Remember, a thought can sometimes trigger fear, which evokes the ego, so your job is to feel it rise and reassure the ego all is well and fine and you are safe. You are in control. You don't need the ego to come to your rescue any longer like you did as a child.

In baby steps, start speaking and living your truths. For example, I started wearing the clothes I wanted to wear.

This didn't mean I never wore what my husband wanted me to wear, but once I considered what he wanted and what I wanted, I made the final decision.

And not from my wounded ego, not to be difficult, because that would have been from my ego, but because it was my truth. What I wear is a reflection of who I am. I didn't want to wear clothes as a reflection of who he wanted me to be. In the past, most of the time I wore what my husband wanted me to wear because I didn't want conflict; it was just easier. I was not authentic and not living in my truth. It may seem silly, but keep digging to find out when you don't live in your truth because of fear. It could be anything. There are so many situations when we don't speak our truth.

- When haven't you done the things you've chosen to do or spoken your truth? Document them in your notebook.

Think about how you answer people when they ask you something. Do you say exactly your truth, or do you skirt around it from the fear of hurting others? This way of responding comes from our conditioning, not our authentic selves. We were conditioned to believe that to speak our truth would hurt someone, and we wouldn't want to do that—but it is not necessarily true. This is a story handed down for generations. Yes, the truth can hurt, but trust me, a lie hurts a lot more for a lot longer and is very confusing to others.

When you go into fear, watch what happens and observe it. Feel it. We are flushing our egos out into the open to see why we have gone into fear and what we are actually truly afraid of. Our fears can only be healed using the courage to go toward them and build this awareness.

For instance, when I was choosing my clothes, I chose what I wanted to wear and endured my partner not always being happy with my decisions. I asked him to respect my choices. What I wear is a reflection of my personality, and I was learning to find out who I was again, void of others' opinions.

I found out his belief was "If you don't wear what I want you to, it feels like you don't love me." Neither his fear nor his story was mine, but it used to control me. His wound was "not being considered." This came from his years as a young boy growing up at home with a father who was clearly very wounded himself and could not show his children love.

This is the work awareness uncovers—whose wound is it? Taking action creates experiences for you to cultivate the courage to live in your truth. This work is about facing your fears. The most courage you will ever need is to stand up to yourself. When you get through this book, you will understand that all this time the awareness you need has all been inside you—none of this is happening outside of you. It feels as though it is, but your own conditioning and fears have created your reality. The good news: you can change your thoughts to align with this new understanding and thereby create a new reality without fears.

Courage to be Vulnerable

Until you become courageous enough to expose all of yourself, you will not learn who you really are. Every part of yourself needs to come out from your protective shell, from hiding. I call this "flushing out." I remember when I was sixteen, I felt flushed out. I had not been in a relationship yet, so I never felt the need to compromise myself, or to manipulate to find peace, because I could create that for myself. You can imagine as I entered this exciting time, finding someone to share my life with, I had no idea what I was walking into because of the way I had been conditioned to be in a relationship from watching my own mother. My mother communicated (in her relationship) from a place of fear, of trying to keep the peace, and therefore didn't speak her truth. And so I learned this way too. She said yes when she meant no.

EXERCISE VII

Write down a vision of who you were at the age of sixteen. What were your aspirations? What did you spend your days doing? Did you feel free to be yourself at this time? What age were you when you last remember feeling the freedom to be you?

This step is about opening yourself up to be even more vulnerable, and speaking your truth is how to do this. Start with small things. Make a list of the things you say or do that don't align with your true self—they're things you say and do to keep the peace or avoid conflict, or to control what you want. You're testing the waters of how you can learn to feel safe through the experience of speaking your truth.

Don't judge what you write down or do; just observe. Remember that judgment—yours and others'—shuts down your evolution. Treat this time as though you were an inquisitive child.

When you start opening up to speak your truth, ground your energy. Bring your awareness into your feet and feel rooted in the earth; be solid like a thick tree trunk that can't blow over in a storm. The storm will come, but the objective is that you will still be standing after it passes. The only way to know this for sure is to stand in the storm. Tell yourself you are safe and not afraid; breathe. This will take practice.

Remind yourself you are a spiritual being having a human experience. You are not learning anything new. In fact, you are remembering the truth of who you are and realizing the delusion you have been living under. Fear is an illusion; don't let fear stop you from speaking your truth. This is the way to uncover your true self and set yourself free. The road to freedom is through truth. Be like the eye of the hurricane—in the center it is calm.

Why is it important to become conscious of these things? Because until you are aware of your actions and honest with why you do what you do, it's impossible to love yourself unconditionally. Awareness of self brings love of self. Once you can do this, you can love others the same way, and this is how we will create heaven on Earth.

I'm going to reiterate what I said before about fear and what physically happens to our bodies when we are feeling fear. You will feel what I describe below in your own body when you start to speak your truth. I want to prepare you to watch it in yourself.

Physical Reaction to Fear

Your physical body releases chemicals when it senses a threat, fear. Adrenaline gets released into your body, and this makes you feel a rush and induces a heightened awareness. Just breathe, while allowing feelings to move through you. Know the adrenaline will dissipate in ninety seconds or so, and you will feel less fear. Be kind to yourself. You are learning to stand in your own power and truth, and that takes practice and courage.

If you are prone to anxiety attacks or panic attacks, this is what's happening to you. You had a thought, which created fear, which called up the ego protector, and this physically called on the body to respond with adrenaline, which resulted in an anxiety attack that felt like you were out of control. This feeling is what's frightening you, but believe me, it will pass once you bring awareness to why it's happening and understand it.

Be patient and know this is happening. Wait and breathe for ninety seconds, again allowing your feelings to move through you. You will see you can control this physical reaction. It simply was a manifestation of a perceived threat that put you into fear. You created it from your unconsciousness, therefore you can change it. This is being conscious and understanding the energy and what's happening in your body. You only become afraid if you feel out of control; knowing you can control this because you now understand helps you feel back in control and out of fear. You must enter into the fear, become one with this awareness of fear, to have the experience to know you will be fine. Experience creates awareness, which allows consciousness to evolve.

Imagine if we were all taught that this natural sensation is part of the body's protective mechanism, that we all have it. The body doesn't know the difference between a lion about to eat you and an assertive voice about to engage in a conflict with you. Either way, the body's response is the same. Because of this lack of understanding, we have not allowed ourselves to go into this fear; it feels too big. At times it feels like life or death. It can be very scary indeed, hence panic attacks.

I still remember when, as a little girl in Grade 5, I forgot my lunch one day. The teacher called me to the front of the room and I felt humiliated by her and shamed. She wasn't aware how sensitive I was. From this seemingly small incident, I became super shy, hiding myself throughout school, not wanting to be seen. I was embarrassed and hurt from the incident. She didn't know how I felt, but my story started. I felt shame and I hid myself. Looking back, I understand it as a wound I stored from an experience I had as a child. Today as an adult I can let it go because I understand it as an old hurt from a time when I was vulnerable and afraid and didn't understand.

There is a lot of different interpretations of what vulnerability is. For the purpose of this work, vulnerability is the ability to believe beyond your feelings of fear that you are safe, and in this safe place you can now release all your thoughts you have been holding onto.

EXERCISE VIII

Allow yourself to be vulnerable to whatever you are watching yourself do; do it anyway and do not judge. Write down your feelings and experiences about being vulnerable and how it made you feel.

Until we are prepared to see all sides of ourselves, we cannot choose differently. We must first become aware of how we act. We are afraid to be vulnerable and expose ourselves. What if what we find out about ourselves, we don't like? What if we realize we have been acting out of our own fears? It's a necessary step, and we must expose all of ourselves until there is nothing left to hide. We must grow to love all of ourselves—whatever we find out.

Forgiveness is a wonderful thing. Until you become aware, you don't know what you are responsible for, and when you find out, you can forgive yourself and let go (we will discuss this more in the following chapter). For example, it's better to find out you don't like the way you act with certain people sometimes. I'm suggesting you work toward awareness to find out why certain people trigger you because this is about your healing, not theirs. They may do or say something that annoys you; the question is why does it annoy you? What are you feeling?

EXERCISE IX

Write down a time when you felt like this and why you think you were triggered.

I'm not suggesting at this time that you have to say anything to that person. I'm just trying to make sure you become aware of what triggers you. The exercise is to learn to love that part of yourself, too. The parts you have judged in the past need to be forgiven. Judgment shuts down our evolution of yourself and other. Families make great catalysts for this work because they can be our biggest triggers.

Ego Awareness

You are now becoming aware there are two of you. One is the doer and one is the witness to the doer. Watch the doer. When the witness (observer) and the doer become fully aware of each other, then you will have reached conscious awareness. The doer is reacting from wounds of the past; it is referred to as a *wounded ego* or *shadow personality*. This is what we are trying to heal through our awareness—the reactor within us is triggered by the wounds of our past. Bringing awareness to our triggers tells us we have not yet healed a wound and therefore we know we must dig deeper.

Eckhart Tolle in his book *A New Earth* teaches us about the ego in depth. I highly recommend this book as part of this practice. Eckhart teaches us from his own experience, sharing his observations about what the ego is, why we have it, and how we can integrate it into our own lives. This is step one, becoming aware of the ego, the duality within us.

When you are in communication with another person, become aware of their body's energy and yours. Ask yourself, "What am I feeling?" If you're afraid, ask yourself, "Is this their fear or mine?" This is learning to understand what is yours and what is the other person's.

Be conscious of what is happening in the energy. Ask, "How do I stay on my own compass course and not get pulled onto others'?" You stay on your own compass course by not going into fear. This happens when you start loving and trusting yourself.

When you release fear, others will feel it even if you haven't spoken a word. Be mindful of your thoughts. It is much better to verbally communicate you are feeling fear, as this then becomes less confusing to the other person. If you are in fear and don't say anything, the other person may also go into fear, not knowing what the fear is all about or whose it is. It creates confusion. Have the courage to say, "I'm in fear about something. I haven't identified it yet, but I can feel it rising up in me." In this statement, I would be detached from the outcome—no shame, no judgment on me, just building awareness and stepping into vulnerability. People will respond to this with compassion toward you because they have not been triggered by your fear.

Starting the conversation this way takes you into being totally responsible for your own energy and allows other people to understand that fear is in you. They can just wait and be present for what comes next. When you feel afraid, instead of trying to run away to find a "better" place, stand with the fear. Stand still, be with it in the moment; the fear will show you what needs to happen. Allow the fear to surface and show itself. It does feel frightening, though. I encourage you to trust and allow your fear to surface, because it is communicating with you. It will tell you what it needs once you give it the chance and the platform.

Healing into Consciousness

The wounded ego is created as a result of hurts and past events from your life, and perhaps even from many lifetimes. It is difficult to uncover when and where these wounds came from, yet they have become part of you. You will hear some people say "It's just my personality. It's the way I am." In truth, that's not true. If you are in reaction, it's because you are wounded, and your responsibility is to find out what that wound is. Bring awareness and allow the transformation into consciousness so the energy can exit your body. This is healing into consciousness.

I had several experiences like this in my evolution into consciousness. One experience was particularly scary. It frightened me at the time, as I did not understand it, but what I have come to know is that I released wounds of the past. With this release I felt the energy surge through my body as it shook, which continued until my body relaxed. I knew it had moved through me and was gone. I wasn't triggered any longer from this wound. Most of the time my experience was more like a holding pattern. This time I was shaking. I was conscious of the energy leaving me, but both can happen. Energy leaves you when you give it a voice, a platform—it's healing, not hurting. Because of this fear we feel, we often shy away from dealing with our own pain and hurt. We have not built a platform for this to be released from the body. These tools will become your compass that leads you home to yourself.

Tip

If you find yourself judging or irritable with others because of how they behave or what they say, ask yourself why you are thinking these thoughts? There is always an answer: you just have to enquire within yourself why you're disappointed in them. Our perspective on any given issue is what causes us the pain. It's not what happens to us, it's how we react to what happens to us that creates our reality.

If you are a person who likes to give advice, but it isn't always received with thanks, and this confuses you, try this when in communication with friends and family. Instead of giving people advice, ask them questions that are genuinely enquiring that are meant to be a gift to the other person, rather than an attempt to persuade them of your own viewpoint. This works well because the ego doesn't go into fear and helps lead that person to their truth. You may have noticed that sometimes when you give advice, the other person's ego gets triggered. This is because they have a fear of not being in control. So instead of offering advice, try rephrasing and ask questions. This way the ego is less likely to get triggered, and instead the person goes within to seek the answer. This creates more awareness, less fear, and more love, and is truly helpful.

Forgiveness

Can you think of a person or an experience that you have never forgiven? Most people at some point refuse to forgive a person or an event, and this is very damaging to themselves. What they don't understand is forgiveness is not for other people—it is for the trapped energy to be released from themselves. Without forgiving others, this cannot happen, and your wound will stay forever trapped in your body. You will be triggered every time something happens in your life that taps into the wound. Saying "I forgive you." is powerful. You will feel a sensation arise in your body. This is the pain you have been holding onto. You don't have to forgive the action but you do have to find a way to forgive the person otherwise you will keep the energy trapped within you. It may take a few attempts before you authentically reach it, but you will. Keep trying.

There is a higher intelligence at work—call it guardian angels, call it God, call it the collective universal intelligence, call it whatever you wish—but know you are being helped in this life. You just need to have faith. Open your eyes and heart, and you will see the signs. Whenever people are stuck on how to forgive, I share this poem and exercise, sometimes more than once. You will know the hurt has left you when this poem no longer carries emotions while you're reading it. Don't forget, sometimes we also need to forgive ourselves. Be sure to use it for that, too.

EXERCISE X

The poet's name is Helen Belot and she instructs you to do the following:

- Prepare a special place (outside or inside) and make sure you have at least an hour. If you're inside, burn candles, incense, etc., and play some of your favorite music.

- Take a blank page and write down all the names of people who have hurt you, made you angry, frustrated or upset you. Also, note why or how. Don't forget to include yourself.

- Imagine all these people gathered around you, and when they are all present (including yourself), speak the following words to them. While you do so, imagine them listening, reacting with a smile, thanking you, and leaving quietly.

A little warning about this next step: I suggest reading this poem only when you are ready to sit down with it, rather than reading it through as part of the book. I am very quick to go into the energy, so for me I wait to do this step when I have the hour as recommended.

Forgiveness

I do not know why
You did what you did
And I do not know why
You said what you said
I do not know why
You are the way you are
But I accept that is where
You need to be just now
And I forgive you, and
I forgive myself
I release all anger, bitterness and resentment
Past and present
And I forgive you, and
I forgive myself
And I release both of us
In my love
And so be it
I now easily release all resistance
The past has no power over me
I am the only person that thinks in my mind

My mind is powerful
I now choose thoughts that free me
I trust myself to release and let go
I am powerful and safe and secure
I am free ... I forgive everyone
I forgive myself ... I forgive the past
And by doing so ... I am free
I am free ... I am free
I FORGIVE EVERYONE
I FORGIVE MYSELF
I FORGIVE ALL PAST EXPERIENCES
FORGIVING EVERYONE ... FORGIVING
MYSELF
I AM FREE ... I AM FREE.

Helen Belot is a Sekhem master now living in Australia. This is a powerful ancient Egyptian healing method. She works toward global healing. I participated in a Level 1 and 2 Sekhem energy workshop in 2009 on Salt Spring Island with an instructor of her philosophy. When your heart and mind are aligned with conscious-compassionate choices, healing takes place. If you are searching for healing in your life, it will always include forgiveness.

Try to lighten up the heaviness of this work by realizing that one day you will feel the weight lifted from your shoulders and life will be light again. Treat it like people who have agreed to be detectives in each other's lives and are helping to solve the puzzle of healing. Ask each other, "What are you afraid of?" Partners, friends, or any type of counselor can be helpful but are not required. For me, I chose to take the solo road. It's the hardest road, because you feel alone and you keep getting stuck in your own head, but for me it was the perfect road for my own evolution. I'm sure it took me longer, but remember, I felt shame and wanted to stay in hiding.

In Relationships

Speak your truth. If others don't want to be a part of this journey, that's okay. My partner didn't want to participate in the beginning. Just know one day others will know and understand why it is so important for you to speak your truth. No one else has to do anything for you to do your work. This is about personal responsibility, and if you do your work and they (partners, family, friends, etc.) don't—that's okay. You will see why as you evolve. Don't get caught in the trap of thinking others have to do something as well. That was my trap, my own ego.

Many people think, "Well, if they are not willing to do their work, then we don't have a relationship." Maybe that will be right, but also consider that they were chosen to be in your life for you to evolve, just as you were chosen to be in theirs, and leave it at that for now. Or perhaps you both chose each other. Trust there is a bigger plan at play. We are in each other's lives sometimes for a lifetime, sometimes for a short while. It is the ego that makes up the story that others have to do the work too. This is not true; this work is about personal responsibility.

Others don't have to do anything for you to evolve. This is your journey—a journey all must walk if they want to reach and discover their authentic selves and be free to be themselves.

Throughout this work, write down observations about yourself and own up to them. Your life is your personal responsibility. I had to own up to things that I did. As I see it, that's the only way to truly accept ourselves. If you did things you're not proud of, you did them out of fear and were unaware at the time. Forgive yourself. There's no shame and no blame.

Remember, I lied and manipulated to keep the peace. This understanding was hard to swallow at the time, but it freed me. My sister, who had tendencies to bully others, went through this work, which was super hard for her, too, but it also freed her to be her authentic self and love herself.

You can share your findings with others only after you have an understanding of these steps and feel secure that you won't allow others to confuse you. If you're too new at this practice and you share with others too soon, their wounded egos might try to pull you back into old beliefs. They have fears they don't want to face, and if you face your fears, then it could be a threat to their wounded egos.

I'm referring to friends and family because society has conditioned us with beliefs that simply have not been helpful, and we have allowed them to unconsciously influence us. Many people may try to talk you out of this journey, because they like the way things are, they don't want you to change. However, this is all about what you want. You are on a journey to discover the truth of yourself. You are here now, so this means you are ready.

Forgiveness of self and others means you have come to understand that we can only act/react from where our level of consciousness is at any given moment. This understanding brings in a level of compassion.

STEP SEVEN

Asking Others for Help

At this point you may have been working on this practice for four months, four years, or more—time doesn't matter. What matters is that you are working your way to complete authenticity and speaking your truth, to reach one-hundred-percent awareness of self and to create the life you want. This means you have become aware of yourself and your triggers, and you can now transform your fear to love.

I remember watching an interview with Eckhart Tolle in which he was asked, "So does this mean you don't have an ego?" His answer was "I am human, therefore I have an ego, but instead of the awareness of my ego being a long way away before I recognize it, now it's just a couple of seconds away, and I just breathe and know that I am fine." (I believe this was during the ten-part Eckhart workshop Oprah created. You can find it here on Vimeo. It's a great introduction to his work.)

Once you have come this far and understand the need for you to know how you have been communicating, ask others for their help. This is a big step, because you have to be prepared for what they say with detachment. Remember, it's not for you to defend or react or even respond—this is only their truth, not necessarily "the truth"—that is for you to review and ponder on. They have to feel safe enough and know you are ready to hear their truth in response to your questions, without going into fear. Knowing how others perceive you will help you become consciously aware of how you act. Find out how you are received by others when you communicate. This could be a bit of a shock. Don't judge it: become aware so you can continue to do your inner work on a deeper level.

EXERCISE XI

Ask people in your daily circle, or those close to you, to help you become even more aware of how you communicate. Let them know you would like to communicate your truth better—with respect and compassion. For this to happen, you would like to ask them questions about yourself. Ask them to answer with respect and compassion, and most of all, from their truth. This is key. Be clear: you don't want them to give an answer to make you feel better—that is not helpful. Make note of each person's answers in your notebook to reflect back on.

- How do you feel when we are together?
- Do I give you energy or take your energy? If only sometimes, explain.
- Am I a good listener or do you feel I am preoccupied with my own agenda?
- Am I someone you look forward to spending time with or not? If only sometimes, why?
- Do you feel we are equally able to give and take within our relationship, or am I taking more than I am giving?
- Can you speak your truth with me? Or are you afraid to talk to me about some things because you are afraid of my reactions?
- Have you felt I defend myself? If yes, can you give me an examples?
- When I react, do you feel you can bring that to my attention or not?
- Do you believe I am okay with being wrong, or do you feel that is a reaction of mine?
- Most of the time, would you describe me as coming from a place of love or fear? If fear, what topics do you feel trigger me?

- Do I tend to be negative or judgmental of others?
- Please feel free to comment, respectfully and compassionately, with any observations you have of me while I communicate with you or you witness me with others.

I suggest you print off the questions for them to fill out when they're not in your presence and hand back to you when they are done. If they would rather be with you, then that is fine, too. I just want to make sure they are not in fear when answering the questions. It's also not a discussion as much as it is a research exercise.

Thank those who participated in the exercise for their honesty and assure them this is about building awareness in communication and you appreciate their truth. Make sure they know this is not to make you feel better—you are simply asking for their truth when in communication with you. Once you have completed this exercise, it will be apparent that you are not necessarily perceived by others as you perceive yourself, and in this awareness will unfold.

So often we believe we are one person. We have a story in our heads about who we are out in the world and how we are perceived. But this inquiry into self often shows us we are not always received the way we believe we are. I remember when a friend of mine once said I had not been very approachable in my past, but once fear left me I became warm and welcoming. At times, in conversation with others, I was called a bully. Looking back, I realize this was my fear, which was often triggered by another's fear and confused me. I was perceived as a bully because I communicated from fear, not love. My energy attacked instead of expressing what I was feeling in order to help others understand me.

The Seven Steps in Review

Step One: Awareness Using Truth - Learn to identify what you are feeling—love or fear—and how they feel different in your body.

Step Two: Compassion - Once you've identified what you're feeling, and built awareness, you can work on switching from fear to love, and your delivery will naturally become more compassionate.

Step Three: Detachment - Realize you cannot fix anyone else; that is their decision to evolve or not. By becoming aware of your own fear-versus-love energy and having compassion toward others who don't yet understand, you find acceptance and in that, detachment. It no longer becomes about anyone else but yourself.

Step Four: Action - Consciously speak your truth to create an experience with which you can now witness and reflect upon creating a new level of awareness.

Step Five: Courage to be Vulnerable - Find the courage you need to move forward in the action of speaking your truth.

Step Six: Forgiveness - The ego will fight you here; it wants to continue in conflict and blame. Recognize that forgiveness is not for the other person, it's for you and your body to be able to heal from the hurt and pain of the event. Discover the magic of forgiveness. As you forgive, your energy changes and those around you are now feeling this forgiveness also, which is powerful healing work.

Step Seven: Asking Others for Help - Ask people most important to you to help you become more aware of how you communicate. Accept that no judgement or defence on your part can be present. This is a research step not to be discussed with by the person who answered your questions but just for you to decide what those responses mean for you going forward.

What I've Come to Know

- Using Truth as your compass creates an experience that opens the door into your wounded self for you to choose to heal.

- Delivering your truth with compassion dissipates fear in others so you can evolve in your own truth and therefore so can others.

- Following your joy will get you on the path to being you.

- We cannot evolve unless we are prepared to release the wounds of our past.

- We communicate from our energy first, before any words are spoken.

- Fear and love are the duality of ourselves.

- The ego is like a scared child still protecting itself, waiting patiently for us to grow up and take care of ourselves. It needs our love and compassion, and it needs us to take responsibility for our lives.

- The quest for unconditional love of self is our priority and why we are here.

- Awareness is the key to consciousness.
- We feed our fears based on the stories we tell ourselves.
- We have the power to change our lives, to build awareness and live as our authentic selves.
- Love and above is the frequency with which we enter grace, a place where we can hear our own intuition and guidance, find our own compass.
- We can create heaven on Earth.

Epilogue

Most people never reach their full potential because of fear. *Smile at Fear: Awakening the True Heart of Bravery* by Chogyam Trungpa has a great paragraph that spoke strongly to me. It helped me climb out of my fear to speak my truth.

"Once there was a young warrior. Her teacher told her that she had to do battle with fear. She didn't want to do that. It seemed too aggressive; it seemed unfriendly. But the teacher said she had to do it and gave her the instructions for the battle. The day arrived. The student warrior stood on one side and fear stood on the other. The warrior was feeling very small, and fear was looking big and wrathful. They both had their weapons. The young warrior roused herself and went toward fear, prostrated three times, and asked, "May I have permission to go into battle with you?" Fear said, "Thank you for showing me so much respect that you ask permission." Then the young warrior said, "How can I defeat you?" Fear replied, "My weapons are that I talk fast, and I get very close to your face. Then you get completely unnerved, and you do whatever I say. If you don't do what I tell you, I have no power. You can listen to me, and you can have respect for me. You can even be convinced by me. But if you don't do what I say, I have no power." In that way, the student warrior learned how to defeat fear."

We give our power away every time we do not stand in our truth. Why? Because when we do not stand in our own truth, we either give someone else permission to control us or we control others, simply because we are afraid.

Many of us are afraid. Some people are afraid to speak their truth for fear of conflict, while others speak their truth and get into conflict because they are afraid of being controlled, but on both counts the real problem underlying this communication is the lack of consciousness within our own choices and fear. We have been making choices in our lives from an unconscious place. We tend to make choices based on a safe, protective outcome and on what we believe we need to help keep us safe, not on what our truth really is.

Historically, we have grown through generations of wars and conflicts. War is still rooted in the fear of something. Imagine a world in which we could communicate without being in fear for our safety. In our daily lives, we are in survival mode. We are in fear for our lives when in truth we are fine, but because we hold this belief, it has become our reality.

My father was explosive. My mother believed a war was going to happen every time he raised his voice. She sent us off to bed to avoid the flying bullets. In fact, I never saw it that way, but because my mother created this belief in me, it eventually became my reality, too, until the day I had this awakening. There isn't any war against me, there's only the one inside my head. I am made from love. I am lovable and I love others and myself—unconditionally. None of the people in my life need to be anything other than what they are for me to love them. They're on a journey, just like me. If I judge them—then I judge myself. As I said before, judgment stops our evolution. There is nothing wrong; all is as it should be. We are spiritual beings learning to be human.

There is intimacy in conflict. I had to learn and understand this.

There is magic in this work. I have seen it unfold. As I surrendered to my truths, so did those around me, and, it seemed, with little effort on their part.

I created a vibrational shift into unconditional love for myself, and doing so magically affected others the same way. I ask, "If there were only me, if I were the only person in the world, what would I do?" If this question is the one I continue to answer to learn what my truth is (and if I live by my truth), I can answer without fear. I am in fact acting from love, creating love on our planet, and from that frequency great healing is possible.

I did all this for myself, without any expectations of anyone else. No one had to agree with me, no one had to come on the journey with me. However, living my life in the truth of who I am … I am free and happy to share with all of you! So, my fellow fearless warriors, I wish you well wherever this journey takes you, and my hope is that you, too, become all of who you came to be in this lifetime and share the love that you are.

It is easier for me now. My stories have gone quiet and I live a joyful life. I'm just so happy to be able to share my experiences with all of you. I know for sure that *at love and above* you will feel the shift. Be brave, be diligent, have no judgment. Truth delivered with compassion will lead you home to yourself and back to love and above. Trust the energy.

We believe we can make a difference in the world by helping others, though we must be careful with this belief. I believe that without conscious awareness of oneself first, this may not be the case. I called myself the "unconscious peacekeeper" because before I became conscious, I was actually creating the mini-wars in my own world, believing I was helping others. I was unaware of my fears.

My hope in releasing this book is that you will learn to follow your true compass also. Please pass this book on to another when you have practiced to the point at which it has become natural for you to allow yourself to be truly you. Or share this book with others so they might take this courageous journey also. Start your own love revolution!

Thank you for stepping into your courage to participate in creating the best life ever. Your contribution to yourself will have an effect on our wounded world and, one person at a time, we can heal.

Your compass awaits you.

Love,
Chental x

It's time!
Speak your truth, deliver it fearlessly
and with compassion, and change
will happen.

Suggested Reading

A New Earth: Awakening to Your Life's Purpose
Eckhart Tolle
ISBN 978-0-452-28996-3
www.eckharttolle.com

After working through Eckhart's books, I understood what the ego is, why we have it, and why we need to become conscious of it to heal and integrate it. Oprah describes his work as "a wake-up call for the entire planet, one reader at a time."

Eckhart explains our minds in such a way that it all makes sense. I learned why it's important to awaken to my life purpose and follow my own compass. I always used to wonder, if God made me in his own image, why did I become someone I was not? I finally understood why and where I had lost my way.

Can I Be Me, Without Losing You?
Chental Wilson
ISBN 978-1-5043-5443-1
www.chentalwilson.com

This is my first book. It describes in detail the awakening I experienced, and how I stepped into my truth. I delve into how this transformation affected my relationships, especially my marriage. I took a whole year off work, and I listened and heard the steps I needed to take. I knew the version of myself I had been showing the world wasn't my truth, and I had to make changes, even if it meant losing those I love. Women especially have been conditioned to hide their true selves in the name of peace, but we need to understand that it is not helping, its hurting.

In Search of the Miraculous: Healing into Consciousness
Eliza Mada Dalian
ISBN 978-0-9738773-3-5
Workbook and 2-CD set: ISBN 978-0-9738773-5-9
www.madadalian.com

Spiritual healer Eliza Mada Dalian wrote this book based on her own experiences and teachings. I recommend reading her book as part of the practice of bringing awareness to your wounds and allowing the transformation into consciousness so that the fear can be released from your body. This is healing into consciousness.

There is so much in this book that explains how to release our wounded selves. I refer to this material and the tools in this book many times, because I believe in her message. When you have the courage to allow an experience, you open up the awareness and allow consciousness to come in. This is the work Eliza Mada Dalian is doing with her DHM, the Dalian Healing Method.

Mada Dalian works with the breath, our feelings, our hearts (the feminine). Her work creates an experience for us to feel the wounded energy that Eckhart teaches us about. Through the breath, she brings rise to the wounded ego and helps us transform it, and the energy leaves our bodies for good. Mada's experiential work leaves you feeling relaxed, connected, and free, one wound at a time. It's a gift that keeps on giving, because, remember, our energy affects everyone around us and when we are vibrating at love and above, people can feel it. Mada's teachings awaken us to the truth that "I am what I have been searching for." It's time to love ourselves again.

Additional Texts

These are a few additional publications that I highly recommend when you are learning to use your truth to follow your own compass.

You Can Heal Your Life
Louise Hay
ISBN 978-0-937611-01-2
www.louisehay.com

Power Versus Force
David R. Hawkins, M.D., Ph.D
ISBN 1-56170-933-6

Dying To Be Me
Anita Moorjani
ISBN 978-1-4019-3751-5
https://anitamoorjani.com/

The Biology of Belief
Bruce H. Lipton. Ph.D
ISBN 978-1-4019-4891-7
www.brucelipton.com

What I know for sure is that this group of writers helped awaken in me the truth that I am what I have been searching for, and I am eternally grateful to them all for having the courage to follow their true compasses.

About the Author

Born in High Wycombe, England, into a strong Catholic family, Chental is the second youngest of nine girls. She met her husband at the age of fifteen and was married at nineteen. After thirty-one years of marriage and twenty-eight years of being in the family business, she decided that there must be more for her to learn. As a wife and a mother, she realized that somewhere in between she had left part of herself behind and now she needed to find herself again. Today she lives in British Columbia with her husband. This is her second book.

Chental's first book, *Can I Be Me Without Losing You?* (ISBN 978-1-5043-5443-1), is a journey into self within a relationship. Published by Balboa Press in June 2016, it can be ordered from the website below, amazon.ca, amazon.com, Barnes & Noble, or a number of local bookstores. To receive the most recent version, search by ISBN.

Chental is available for interviews and speaking engagements worldwide and for private coaching via Skype, telephone or in person. She lives in B.C.,

Canada. Contact Chental at chentalwilson@gmail.com for further information.

Follow Chental

Facebook: Chental Wilson: The Consciousness Coach

Websites: chentalwilson.com

Instagram: @chentalwilson

Amazon Review Request

If you have found this book helpful, please let others know about it. I would really appreciate a review on Amazon, as this helps get my message out to all who would benefit from learning how to speak their truth and deliver it with compassion.

Thanks so much for spending time reading *Pure Pilgrimage*. If you would like to continue the discussions, I would love for you to join me and others on our Facebook page: Chental Wilson: The Consciousness Coach

Thanks again,
Chental x

56001981R00071

Made in the USA
Columbia, SC
20 April 2019